The Collector's Series / Volume 7

LOUISIANA
Creole
&Cajun

by
Margaret Maring

D0094637

The
AMERICAN
★COOKING★
GUILD™

Boynton Beach, Florida

Dedication
To my husband Gary, for his never-ending love and support for everything that I do; to our wonderful children Greg, Eric and Laura, who have often had less than elegant dinners on nights I have gone off to teach others about cooking; to my lifelong friend, Betty Lou, for all of her help and sharing of recipes; and to my dear brother Roderick, who loves the food from the land of his birth and who has helped spread those traditions to the west coast, as I have to the east coast.

Acknowledgments
—Cover Design and Layout by Pearl & Associates, Inc.
—Cover Photo by Burwell and Burwell
—Edited by Martina Boudreau
—Illustrations by Jean Brill Hough
—Typesetting/Layout by Catharine Hocker

More...Quick Recipes for Creative Cooking!
The American Cooking Guild's *Collector's Series* includes over 30 popular cooking topics such as Barbeque, Breakfast & Brunches, Chicken, Cookies, Hors d' Oeuvres, Seafood, Tea, Coffee, Pasta, Pizza, Salads, Italian and many more. Each book contains more than 50 selected recipes. For a catalog of these and many other full sized cookbooks, send $1 to the address below and a coupon will be included for $1 off your first order.

Cookbooks Make Great Premiums!
The American Cooking Guild has been the premier publisher of private label and custom cookbooks since 1981. Retailers, manufacturers, and food companies have all chosen The American Cooking Guild to publish their premium and promotional cookbooks. For further information on our special market programs, please contact the address below.

The American Cooking Guild
3600-K South Congress Avenue
Boynton Beach, FL 33426

Table of Contents

Introduction

Writing this book of Creole and Cajun cooking has been a great pleasure because it has brought back so many special memories of happy days in Louisiana. It was a very simple book to write since most of the recipes have come from my cooking classes in Montgomery County, Maryland (just outside of Washington, D.C.) where I have taught for the past eleven years. Although I have taught many different cooking classes, my favorites are the classes in Creole and Cajun cooking. The enthusiasm of my students as I have introduced them to the delights of the foods from south Louisiana has been a real joy to me. I am happy to share some of these recipes, as well as my thoughts on cooking in the Creole and Cajun styles, with you.

Now you too will be able to recreate some of the New Orleans elegance, some of the warm Cajun hospitality, and some of the "good ole down home southern cooking" that is represented in this book. Enjoy!

An Historical Perspective

When New Orleans is mentioned, many things often come to mind. For some, it may be the excitement of the French Quarter, the carnival festivities of Mardi Gras, the beautiful homes of the Garden District, or the mighty Mississippi and riverboats. For those who have been fortunate enough to eat there, thoughts turn to the wonderful Creole and Cajun cooking.

Louisiana has a rich and interesting history, which still affects her traditions and cuisine today. People with diverse backgrounds came to Louisiana and called it home, bringing with them the rich heritages of their homelands. She offered to them a dowry of seafood, fish, game, spices, nuts, and vegetables.

The Creoles

The French founders of Louisiana arrived at the end of the 1600's. French culture was strongly entrenched when, in 1765, Spain took possession of Louisiana. Marriage between the Spanish and the French was inevitable but the customs remained predominantly French. Life was formal and full of tradition. The Spaniards gave the Creoles their name, "Criollo", for "children born in the colonies".

The French planted the seeds for Creole cooking, but it was cultivated and fertilized by the Spaniards, the Africans, and the native Choctaw Indians. The result was a happy marriage of cultures and cuisines. Creole meals were often formal. The city cooks of New Orleans gave attention to presentation with an air of sophistication.

The Cajuns

In the early 1600's French peasants settled in Acadia, Nova Scotia. In the mid 1700's when Britain acquired Canada, many of these French loyalists were forced to leave Canada, and south Louisiana became their new homeland. Their descendants are called Cajuns, which is derived from the word Acadian.

Cajun cooking was casual cooking of the country, often spicier than Creole and characterized by dishes cooked in one pot. The philosophy of a Cajun cook was that of generosity—there was always room for more.

Today, many Creole and Cajun dishes have become intertwined. South Louisiana offers the finest of food and drink extended with a warm welcome in the Louisiana Bayou Country. The Cajun and Creole recipes are the basis for many of the famous dishes served in fine New Orleans restaurants.

Success in Cooking

With any type of cooking, it is important to buy the freshest and the best quality ingredients that can be found. The understanding of basic fundamentals and technique is important to assure the success of Creole and Cajun cooking. There are some ingredients that I always use fresh: lemon juice, grated Parmesan cheese, grated nutmeg, and garlic. I always use fresh herbs when they are available instead of dried herbs.

Since south Louisiana has many excellent cooks, there are no "set recipes" for the many popular dishes of the region. Cooks have their own best recipes which are altered at whim, or modified according to the ingredients on hand. Recipes are seasoned to taste and not usually prepared from exact measurements.

And First You Make The Roux

The roux is the basis of many Creole and Cajun recipes. It is important to learn how to make it properly.

The nutty brown roux is started with equal amounts of oil and flour. Cook the oil and flour over a low heat in a heavy pan. Stir constantly with a wooden spoon until the flour begins to darken —first to a beautiful golden brown and then, if you are patient, the color will turn to a rich coffee colored brown. The aroma should be "nutty".

A properly made roux can take up to 30 or 40 minutes to make. Do not be impatient and turn the heat up too high, otherwise it will scorch and become unusable. Many cooks who use roux often make up large amounts and store it in the refrigerator.

Spice: A Matter of Personal Taste

Whether or not something is considered spicy is a matter of personal taste. I am always amazed in my classes when evaluating the spiciness of a dish that some feel that it is too spicy or too hot, while others feel it is not spicy enough, and still others claim it is just right.

In general, most Creole and Cajun cooking is very spicy—because it is prepared with onions, green onions, red peppers, Louisiana hot sauce, and a variety of other spices. It is important to season to taste, according to your preference. It is also important to remember that the seasoning of a dish will be toned down when it is served over or mixed with rice.

It is important to note that red hot pepper pods can burn the hands and the eyes. Remember to wash your hands well after handling these peppers.

A Word About Shrimp

In south Louisiana, shrimp are eaten in large quantities... boiled with plenty of seasonings and piled high onto the table where everybody peels their own. It is a land where seafood is plentiful and relatively inexpensive.

You may live where shrimp are not as abundant, and a pound or two of shrimp may be a luxury. Most of the gumbos, jambalayas, and other dishes can be made with a large or small amount of seafood depending on your budget. You can add more vegetables to compensate for less seafood.

When purchasing shrimp, buy them fresh whenever possible. Most of the shrimp that are on ice at your market have been previously frozen. I always buy shrimp in the shell. Peeling them takes extra time but I like them much better than those that are peeled and frozen.

A good "shrimp boil" is essential to properly prepared shrimp. Various regions of the country have their own local spices to add to the water. My favorite (and I have tried many) is a box of whole spices that looks similar to pickling spices, called Zatarain's. This company also makes a liquid seafood seasoning from Louisiana, which is available in specialty food shops in many areas of the country. If you are a seafood lover and enjoy spicy shrimp, I would recommend that you stock up on this spice. If you just can't find Zatarian's® anywhere, you can make your own spice by mixing black pepper, cayenne, bay leaves, mustard seed, and allspice.

Cooking Shrimp

In a stock pot with water, add celery, green onion, salt, lemon, and the shrimp boil (see preceding paragraph). Bring the water to a boil and continue boiling for 5-10 minutes to release the aroma and flavor of the seasonings. The amount of water and cooking time will vary according to the amount of shrimp being cooked.

Drop the shrimp in their shells into the rapidly boiling seasoned water. The water will cease boiling. *Do not let it boil again.* The shrimp will turn pink almost immediately, but this does not necessarily mean that they are done. When they start to cook, the shrimp loose their translucent appearance. This takes place from the outside in. Cut into a shrimp before it is done and you will observe the opaque ring around the outside. When the shrimp are no longer translucent, they are finished.

Allow the temperature of the water to rise again to a simmer, *but do not boil.* The shrimp are ready when they have simmered 2-3 minutes. Drain immediately. If they are to be served chilled, cover with ice at once.

Overcooked shrimp tend to be tough and rubbery. Follow these simple instructions and you will have perfect, tender juicy shrimp every time.

Appetizers & First Courses

Artichoke—Crab Crisps

This is an easy do-ahead appetizer.

- ¹/₂ pound crabmeat
- 6 Tablespoons mayonnaise
- 1 Tablespoon grated onion
- 1 teaspoon fresh lemon juice
- ¹/₂ cup grated Swiss cheese
- 1 loaf firm white bread, sliced
- 1 14-ounce can artichoke hearts, drained and quartered
  paprika

In a medium mixing bowl, mix crabmeat, mayonnaise, onion, lemon juice, and cheese. Refrigerate. Cut two circles from each slice of bread with a cookie cutter. Place a piece of artichoke on each bread circle and top with teaspoon of crab and cheese mixture. At this point you can refrigerate. Sprinkle with paprika and place under broiler until bubbly and lightly browned.
Yield: 40 rounds

Oysters Bienville

Plump, juicy oysters smothered in a spicy cheese and shrimp sauce. I have had non-oyster eaters sample these and ask for more.

Shrimp Boil:
- 1 dozen shrimp
- 2 whole green onions
- 1/2 lemon
- 1 stalk celery, broken into large pieces
- 1 teaspoon salt
- 1/2 teaspoon pepper
- 1 bay leaf

Bienville Sauce:
- 1/4 pound mushrooms, sliced
- 1/4 cup butter plus 2 Tablespoons, divided
- 3 Tablespoons flour
- 1 clove garlic
- 1 Tablespoon finely diced onion
- 1 Tablespoon worcestershire sauce
- 1/4 teaspoon celery seed
- 1 Tablespoon sherry
-    rock salt
-    oyster shells
- 1 1/2 pints oysters
-    Parmesan cheese, freshly grated
-    Hungarian paprika

Cook the shrimp as directed in A Word About Shrimp on page 8, seasoning the water with green onions, lemon, celery, salt, pepper and bay leaf. Drain the shrimp, set aside to cool and then chop them. Save the cooking water for the Bienville Sauce, below.

Bienville Sauce

In a medium saucepan over medium heat, sauté the mushrooms in 2 tablespoons butter for 5 minutes, or until tender. Remove mushrooms from pan and set aside, saving the accumulated mushroom juice.

In a medium saucepan over medium heat, melt remaining butter until it foams. Add flour and cook for 1-2 minutes. Add garlic and onion and cook until soft but not brown.

Stir in worcestershire sauce and celery seed. Pour the reserved liquid from the mushroom sauté into a measuring cup and add reserved liquid from shrimp boil to equal $3/4$ cup. Add to sauce. Cook over medium-high heat until sauce gets thick, stirring frequently. Add mushrooms, chopped shrimp and sherry. Taste for seasoning.

Preheat broiler.

Cover a large jelly roll-type pan with aluminum foil (otherwise, the rock salt will corrode the pan). Cover the pan with rock salt and place the oyster shells in the salt. Place an oyster in each shell and broil for 2 minutes. Drain water off oysters and spoon Bienville sauce onto each oyster. Broil for 2 more minutes. Sprinkle grated cheese and paprika over sauce and broil for 2 more minutes. Serve hot.

Variation: If oyster shells are not available, several oysters can be prepared in broiler-proof ramekins.

Yield: 4-6 as first course (about 20 oysters).

Smoked Oyster Puffs

These can also be made with clams or shrimp.

>   8   *ounces cream cheese*
>   6   *Tablespoons milk*
> $1/4$ *cup minced onions*
> $1/2$ *teaspoon worcestershire sauce*
>   1   *clove garlic, minced*
>   1   *3 $3/4$-ounce can smoked oysters, drained and chopped*
>   1   *loaf firm white bread, sliced*

In a medium mixing bowl, beat the cream cheese, milk, onions, worcestershire sauce, and garlic with an electric mixer until light and fluffy. Fold in the oysters.

Cut two rounds from each slice of bread. Toast on one side and butter the other side. Spread a generous teaspoonful of mixture onto each round, buttered side up.

When ready to serve, place under broiler and toast until mixture is lightly browned and puffed. Serve hot.

Yield: 40-50 puffs

Creole Quenelles Des Crevettes

These shrimp quenelles melt in your mouth. A fabulous first course or a perfect luncheon dish, surprisingly easy to make. For a wonderful luncheon, serve with fresh asparagus and your favorite salad.

2	pounds chilled raw shrimp (save the shells)
2	eggs
1/4	teaspoon hot sauce
2	teaspoons salt
1/2	teaspoon freshly grated nutmeg
	dash cayenne pepper
3	cups heavy cream
2	Tablespoons butter
	boiling salted water

The Cream Sauce

	shrimp shells
5	cups water
2	cups clam juice
2	cups white wine
1	pound fresh mushrooms, finely chopped
1/2	cup butter
8	Tablespoons flour
1 1/2	cups cream or half and half
	salt, pepper, and cayenne to taste

Purée shrimp in a food processor for about 1 minute. Add eggs, hot sauce, salt, nutmeg, and cayenne, and blend for a few seconds. Add cream and blend until the mixture is very thick. It should mound when dropped from a spoon. Chill for at least 30 minutes.

In a large skillet heat water to boiling; add salt and butter. Heat two tablespoons in warm water. These will serve as molds for the quenelles. Scoop the chilled shrimp mixture with one tablespoon and shape on the top with the second spoon. Slip into simmering water and poach for 5 minutes. Remove the poached quenelles to a buttered casserole and arrange them side by side. Continue until all are cooked.

The Cream Sauce

In a large saucepan, bring 5 cups water to a slow boil. Add reserved shrimp shells. Lower heat and simmer the shells for 30 minutes. Strain the water to remove the shells and continue to boil the liquid until it is reduced to 2 cups. Add the clam juice and white wine and continue boiling to reduce the liquid to about 3 cups.

Preheat oven to 425°. In a medium saucepan, sauté mushrooms in the butter. Add flour, stirring constantly; cook for 2-3 minutes. Whisk in the 3 cups of reduced liquid, bring to a boil and simmer for 5 minutes. Add the cream and continue to cook until thickened. Season to taste. Pour this sauce over the quenelles in the casserole and bake 20-25 minutes or until the sauce is bubbling and the quenelles have expanded. The poached quenelles may be frozen. Just thaw, cover with sauce, and heat as directed above.

Yield: 10 first course servings.

Sausage Cheese Balls

Keep these in the freezer and use as needed.

    8 ounces sharp cheddar cheese, grated
    1 pound hot bulk sausage
    2 cups baking mix

Place cheese, sausage, and baking mix in a large mixing bowl. Work until well mixed. Shape into small balls.

Place on ungreased cookie sheet and bake at 375° until lightly browned, about 10 to 15 minutes. Serve hot. These may be frozen and reheated in a 350° oven until hot.

Yield: approximately 100

Bacon-Oyster Bites

These are quick and easy to make and can be made when oysters are not in season.

- 8 slices bacon, halved
- 1 5-ounce can smoked oysters, drained and chopped
- 1/2 cup herb-seasoned bread stuffing mix
- 1/4 cup water

Preheat oven to 350°.

In a medium frying pan, sauté the bacon until limp and partially cooked.

In a medium mixing bowl, combine the oysters, herb stuffing mix and water. Stir well. Shape mixture into small balls, using one tablespoon of mixture for each. Wrap a half slice of bacon around each ball and secure with a toothpick. Place balls in a shallow baking pan and bake at 350° for 25-30 minutes.

Yield: 16 bite-sized balls.

Pecan Cheese Crisps

This dough can also be put into a cookie gun to make cheese straws.

- 6-8 Tablespoons soft butter
- 2 cups grated extra sharp cheddar cheese, at room temperature
- 1 cup sifted flour
- 2 teaspoons baking powder
- 1 teaspoon salt
- 1/2-1 teaspoon cayenne pepper
- pecan halves

Preheat oven to 325°.

In a medium mixing bowl, cream 6 tablespoons butter with the cheese. Add flour, baking powder, salt and cayenne. If dough is too dry and crumbly add more butter. Form into small balls using 1 teaspoon of dough for each. Press a pecan half into each ball and flatten. Bake on a greased baking sheet until crisp and brown around the edges, about 10 to 15 minutes.

Yield: 50-75 appetizers.

Soups

Bayou Corn Soup with Shrimp

This is especially good in the summer when tomatoes and corn are
fresh.

¹/₄ cup oil
¹/₄ cup flour ·
  1 cup chopped onions
  3 Tablespoons chopped bell pepper
  3 pieces of bacon, fried crisp and chopped
  2 large fresh tomatoes, chopped
1¹/₂ cups fresh corn
  2 quarts water
¹/₄ teaspoon hot sauce, or to taste
     salt and pepper, to taste
  1 pound shrimp, shelled and deveined
  3 Tablespoons parsley, chopped

In a large heavy pot heat the oil and add the flour. Make a light brown
roux as directed on page 7. Add the onions and bell pepper. Cook for
a few minutes until the vegetables are soft but not brown.

Add the bacon, tomatoes, and corn. Cover and cook about 15
minutes over a low heat. Add water, hot sauce, salt and pepper, and
simmer about 40 minutes. Add shrimp and cook slowly for 10
minutes. Sprinkle with parsley and cook 5 minutes.

Yield: 6 servings

Creole Gumbo

Probably south Louisiana's most famous dish, there are almost as many recipes for gumbo as there are cooks in south Louisiana. It is often made with leftovers or whatever is on hand in the kitchen: chicken, sausage, duck, shrimp, or a combination of seafoods. The following is a recipe I've used for years. It may be made with file powder or okra as a thickener, or it may use both. File is made from ground sassafras leaves. It was used by the Choctaw Indians who lived in Louisiana. File is never put into the gumbo until the last minute of cooking. Boiling the gumbo after the file has been added will cause the gumbo to get stringy.

For a casual party, make a big stockpot of gumbo, a big green salad, some crusty garlic bread, a pecan pie and be prepared for a wonderful evening filled with fun and compliments.

> 1   *package chicken parts or 1 chicken*
> 3   *quarts water*
> 1   *rib celery, cut into chunks*
> 2   *whole green onions*
> 1   *bay leaf*
>   *salt and pepper, to taste*
> 4   *Tablespoons flour*
> 4   *Tablespoons oil*
> 1   *cup chopped onion*
> 1   *large bell pepper, chopped*
> 1   *cup chopped celery*
> 1   *cup chopped green onions*
>   *(reserve some for garnish)*
> 2   *cloves garlic, minced*
> 2   *tablespoons butter or oil*
> 1/4   *cup chopped parsley*
> 1   *pound fresh sliced okra (may use frozen)*
>   *salt and pepper, to taste*
> 1/4   *teaspoon cayenne pepper, or to taste*
>   *dash hot sauce, or to taste*
> 1   *teaspoon worcestershire sauce*
> 1   *pound crabmeat*
> 1/2-1   *pound shrimp*
> 1   *Tablespoon file powder*
>   *freshly made fluffy white rice*

Place chicken, water, celery, onions, bay leaf, salt and pepper in a large pot. Cook over medium heat until chicken is tender, about 30-45 minutes.

While chicken is cooking make the roux as directed on page 7. Slowly brown the flour in the oil in a heavy saucepan over a low heat. Stir continually until the flour becomes a dark rich brown. This should take about 30 minutes.

Remove chicken from pot and set aside to cool. Strain the hot chicken broth and taste for seasoning. If necessary, add powdered chicken bullion to the broth to make it stronger. Add the strained broth to the roux while stirring with a wooden spoon.

In a Dutch oven over medium heat, cook the onion, bell pepper, celery, green onions, and garlic in 2 tablespoons butter or oil, until they are soft but not brown. Add to the roux mixture. Add parsley. Stir constantly until smooth and boiling. Add okra, salt, pepper, cayenne, hot sauce, and worcestershire and taste for seasoning. Cook slowly 30 minutes.

While gumbo cooks, debone and dice the chicken. Add chicken to gumbo and cook for 15 minutes. Add the crab and shrimp and cook 3-4 minutes, or until shrimp are done. If you add oysters to the gumbo, add them last and cook only until they crinkle. Remove from heat. Carefully sprinkle in file, stirring gently to prevent file from lumping.

Place rice in individual bowls and top with gumbo. Garnish with chopped green onions. Pass additional file for those who wish to sprinkle it on.

Variation: Add canned chopped tomatoes. Do not add tomatoes if you use oysters, because the tomatoes will cause the oysters to sour.

Yield: 10-12 servings

Oyster Artichoke Soup

An elegant soup in the Creole style, this is probably my favorite soup.

 4 slices bacon, chopped
 4 Tablespoons butter
 2 onions, chopped
 2 stalks celery, chopped
 2 cloves garlic, finely minced
 1 9-ounce package frozen thawed artichoke hearts,
    chopped (or 14-ounce can, drained and rinsed)
15 raw oysters, chopped
 2 Tablespoons flour
 1 bay leaf
 2 pinches thyme
 1 pinch oregano
 2 pinches sweet basil
    sprig fresh rosemary or 1/2 teaspoon dried
 1 Tablespoon Worcestershire sauce
 6 cups water
 2 bunches green onions, chopped
 1 bunch parsley, chopped
1-2 Tablespoons fresh lemon juice
 2 teaspoons paprika
    salt, to taste
    coarsely ground black pepper, to taste
    grated Parmesan cheese, for garnish

In a large saucepan over medium heat, sauté bacon. Remove bacon. Melt butter in bacon fat. Add onions, celery and garlic. Cook until soft but not brown. Add artichokes and oysters. Cook slowly 20-30 minutes.

Add flour and cook 1-2 minutes. Add bay leaf, thyme, oregano, sweet basil, rosemary, Worcestershire sauce, water, green onions and parsley. Bring to boil. Add lemon juice, paprika, salt, and pepper. Taste and adjust seasoning. Simmer for about 30 minutes, partially covered.

When ready to serve, spoon into bowls and sprinkle with Parmesan cheese. Serve with garlic bread, a salad, and your favorite wine.

Yield: 6 servings

Oyster Soup Creole

I like this soup because it is simple and satisfying, and not too rich.

1½ cups finely chopped celery
1½ cups finely chopped green onions
2 cloves garlic, finely chopped
6 Tablespoons unsalted butter
3 Tablespoons flour
6 cups chicken broth, homemade or canned
⅛ teaspoon cayenne
   salt and pepper to taste
1 pint oysters
¼ cup coarsely chopped parsley

In a heavy Dutch oven over medium heat, cook celery, onion, and garlic in butter in a heavy Dutch oven until soft. Stir in flour and cook 2 minutes. Add chicken broth, cayenne, and salt and pepper. Stir until smooth. When it boils, lower the heat and simmer for 30 minutes.

Just before serving stir in the oysters and heat soup for 3 minutes until piping hot. Sprinkle with chopped parsley.

Yield: 6-8 servings

Jean Hough

good. makes a lot (4 people) mom really liked it

Main Dishes

New Orleans
Spinach Crabmeat Casserole

Serve this elegant luncheon dish with broiled tomatoes and crisp bread sticks.

     6   Tablespoons butter
     1   cup chopped onions
    1/4 cup chopped green onions
     2   10-ounce packages frozen chopped spinach,
         thawed and drained
     1   pint sour cream
    1/2 cup freshly grated Parmesan cheese
     1   14-ounce can artichoke hearts, drained
    1/2 teaspoon salt
    1/4 teaspoon pepper
     1   teaspoon worcestershire sauce
    1/4 teaspoon hot sauce
     1   pound crabmeat
    1/2 pound medium-size boiled shrimp

Preheat oven to 350°.

In a heavy skillet over medium heat, melt butter. Add white onions and green onions to skillet and sauté until soft but not brown. Add spinach, sour cream, and cheese. Reduce heat and simmer until heated throughout. Add artichoke hearts, salt, pepper, worcestershire sauce and hot sauce; simmer 2 or 3 minutes. Gently fold in crabmeat and shrimp. Pour into a 2-quart casserole. Bake for 20-30 minutes. Serve hot.

Yield: 6 servings

Trout with Crawfish Sauce

Be flexible with this wonderful dish. If you cannot find crawfish, substitute crabmeat, langostinos or shrimp. It is also good with red snapper or another fish of your choice.

      salt, to taste
      freshly ground black pepper, to taste
3   pounds trout fillets
1   cup sliced onions
6   Tablespoons butter
$^3/_4$ cup dry white wine

Sauce

6   Tablespoons butter
3   Tablespoons flour
1   cup finely chopped green onions
$^1/_4$ cup finely chopped fresh parsley
$^1/_3$ cup chopped celery
1   pound crawfish tails
$^1/_2$ cup heavy cream
$^1/_2$ teaspoon hot sauce
      salt, to taste
$^1/_4$ cup freshly grated Parmesan cheese

Preheat oven to 375°.

Salt and pepper the trout and place in a greased baking dish. Arrange onions on top and dot with butter. Pour wine over all and bake at 375° for 15 minutes, until the fish flakes.

While the fish is baking, make a roux from 4 tablespoons butter and the flour, following the directions on page 7. Stir constantly until it is a light brown. (This will not take as long as the dark roux used for the gumbo and other dishes.) Add the green onions, parsley and celery and sauté until tender. Add the crawfish and cook gently for 5 minutes.

When the fish is done, drain the juices from the baking dish into the crawfish sauce. Stir gently and cook over a low heat until the sauce begins to thicken. Gradually add the cream, hot sauce and salt, blending well. Pour the sauce over the fish and dot with remaining butter. Sprinkle with Parmesan cheese and bake 15 minutes at 375°. Run under the broiler to brown.

Yield: 6 servings

New Orleans Style Bouillabaisse

This bouillabaisse is thick and hearty, more of an entrée than a soup. Use snapper or red fish if you can. Part of the wonderful flavor of this dish comes from rubbing in the spices and garlic. Serve with Spinach Madeline, a salad and crusty French bread for an elegant dinner party.

Fish Stock

	head and bones of a red snapper
1½	quarts water
½	lemon, cut in very thin slices
3	Tablespoons parsley, finely minced
3	bay leaves
1	teaspoon fresh thyme, finely minced
	or ½ teaspoon dried
½	teaspoon salt
½	teaspoon pepper
4	pounds fish fillets
	salt and pepper, to taste
4	cloves garlic, finely minced
	fresh thyme, minced finely (or dried), to taste
	allspice, to taste
	olive oil, to grease pan
3	onions, sliced
⅔	cup sherry
4	cups fresh or canned plum tomatoes, chopped
2	cups fish stock
	salt and pepper, to taste
	cayenne pepper, to taste
1	pound peeled raw shrimp
	pinch saffron
	buttered toast or cooked fluffy white rice

In a large pot place the fish head and fish bones. Add 1½ quarts of water containing sliced lemon, parsley, bay leaf, thyme, salt and pepper. Bring to a boil. When the stock is reduced to 2 cups, remove the head and bones. Strain the stock and reserve.

Rub each slice of the fish with salt and pepper and then with a mixture of garlic, thyme and allspice. Do this with a heavy hand as the fish must be permeated by the seasonings to assure success of this dish. Pour enough olive oil into a large pan to lightly cover the bottom (I usually use a turkey roaster and put it across two burners)

Heat the oil. Add the sliced onion rings over the oil; they will serve as a "rack" to hold the fish. Lay the fish fillets skin side up, over the onions, trying not to have the fillets overlap. Cover and simmer over

continued on next page

medium-low heat for about 10 minutes, turning once so that each side may be partially cooked. The fish will be very tender and may break but that is to be expected.

Remove the fish. Pour off any excess oil. Add the sherry and stir well. Add the tomatoes and 2 cups fish stock. Season to taste with salt, pepper, and cayenne. Let mixture boil until it is reduced by almost one-half. Add shrimp and cook gently 3 minutes; add fish fillets and cook about 5 minutes longer, being careful not to overcook the fish or the shrimp.

Remove approximately one cup of sauce and dissolve a pinch of saffron in the sauce.

To serve, spread saffron sauce over the top of each piece of fish. Place fish on toast or rice; pour sauce over fish and serve immediately.

This can be prepared in advance. Reheat, adding the shrimp and fish during the final 5 minutes of cooking.

Yield: 8-10 servings

Savory Artichoke Chicken Breasts

This is elegant but easy. It does not require much preparation time but the results are special. It is nice served with a green rice casserole.

   1   *9-ounce package frozen artichoke hearts*
 ¹/2 *teaspoon salt*
   4   *chicken breasts, boned*
       freshly ground black pepper
   8   *slices lean bacon*
   4   *Tablespoons sweet vermouth, optional*
   1   *cup chopped canned tomatoes, preferably Italian plum*
   1   *cup sharp Cheddar cheese, grated*

Preheat oven to 350°.

Thaw the artichoke hearts, sprinkle with salt and arrange them on the bottom of a baking dish. Place chicken breasts on top of the artichokes, seasoning lightly with pepper. Lay bacon slices close together over the chicken and spoon vermouth over all.

Bake at 350° for 45 minutes. Drain off excess fat. Combine the tomatoes with the cheese and spoon over the chicken. Cook for 15 more minutes, adding more vermouth if desired. For golden brown color, broil for 1 minute.

Yield: 4 servings

Chicken Rochambeau

Chicken and ham on Holland rusks with mushrooms and topped with Bearnaise Sauce makes a delicious luncheon dish. Nice served with grilled tomatoes.

2	Tablespoons butter
1	cup finely chopped green onions with tops
1-2	cloves garlic, finely chopped
2	Tablespoons flour
2	cups chicken stock, heated
$^1/_2$	cup chopped mushrooms
$^1/_2$	cup dry red wine, Burgundy or Claret
1	Tablespoon worcestershire sauce
$^1/_8$	teaspoon cayenne pepper
	salt to taste
4	chicken breasts, boned
4	Tablespoons flour seasoned with salt and pepper
6	Tablespoons butter
6	Tablespoons oil
4	slices Canadian bacon
4	Holland rusks or toasted English muffins
1	recipe Bearnaise Sauce, page 48

Preheat oven to 350°.

In a large heavy saucepan over medium heat, melt the butter until it foams. Add the green onions and the garlic and cook until they are soft but not brown. Add the flour and cook for 2-3 minutes, stirring constantly with a wooden spoon. Remove from heat and whisk in the hot chicken stock and return to heat and cook until mixture begins to thicken. Add the mushrooms and simmer for 15 minutes.

Add the wine, worcestershire sauce, cayenne, and salt. Cook for 2-3 more minutes and taste for seasoning.

Wash and dry the chicken breasts; coat with the seasoned flour. In a large skillet over medium-high heat, melt the butter and oil. Add floured chicken and sauté until golden brown on all sides. Place in a shallow oven-proof dish and bake at 350° for 20-30 minutes or until done.

Make the Bearnaise Sauce as directed on page 48 (this can be made in advance).

To assemble and serve: Broil the Canadian bacon until hot. Arrange Holland rusks on serving plates. Warm the mushroom sauce. Place a slice of Canadian bacon on each Holland rusk, cover with the mushroom sauce. Place chicken breasts over the sauce and spoon 2-3 Tablespoons Bearnaise sauce over all. Pass extra Bearnaise sauce at the table.

Yield: 4 servings

Oyster Rockefeller Casserole

This is a casserole for Oyster Rockefeller lovers. Need I say more?

1 quart raw oysters
^{1}/2 cup butter
1 rib celery, finely chopped
1 medium onion, finely chopped
^{1}/2 cup finely chopped parsley
1 10-ounce package frozen chopped spinach,
  thawed and drained
^{1}/4 teaspoon anise seed
^{1}/4 cup worcestershire sauce
^{1}/2 cup soft bread crumbs
  salt, to taste
  freshly ground pepper, to taste
  cayenne pepper, to taste
1 cup grated Parmesan cheese
  toasted bread crumbs or cracker crumbs

Preheat oven to 450°.

Grease a casserole dish. Drain oysters and arrange in one layer in the casserole.

In a medium skillet over medium heat, melt butter and sauté celery and onions until they begin to soften. Add parsley, spinach, anise seed, worcestershire, soft bread crumbs, salt, pepper, and cayenne. Spread this mixture over the oysters.

Bake at 450° for 30 minutes. Remove casserole from oven. If necessary, pour off any water that has accumulated from the oysters. Sprinkle with grated cheese and a thin layer of bread or cracker crumbs. Return to oven for 10 minutes or until slightly brown.

Yield: 6 servings

Veal Grillades and Grits

This has traditionally been a breakfast dish in New Orleans, but you might like to serve it for dinner. The delicate veal and the spicy vegetables team up to make a wonderful dish. It is usually served with steaming buttery grits, but can also be served with rice.

4	cloves garlic, minced
1¹/2	pounds veal or beef round, trimmed, cut into thin strips
¹/3	cup flour seasoned with salt and pepper
2	Tablespoons unsalted butter
1	Tablespoon vegetable oil
1¹/2	cups chopped onion
¹/2	cup chopped celery
¹/2	cup chopped green pepper
2	cups canned or fresh plum tomatoes, peeled, seeded, chopped
¹/2	teaspoon dried thyme or 1 teaspoon fresh
¹/2	cup beef broth (may use bouillon cube) salt and freshly ground pepper, to taste hot sauce, to taste
2	cups cooked grits butter, for grits chopped green onion, for garnish

Rub garlic into meat and pound until it has doubled in size. Place the meat into a plastic or paper bag and shake with the seasoned flour.

Heat butter and oil in heavy Dutch oven over medium-high heat. Fry the meat until it is browned, adding more oil if necessary. Transfer meat to a plate and keep warm.

Add onion, celery, and green pepper to the Dutch oven and cook until the vegetables are soft. Add tomatoes, thyme, beef broth and veal or beef. Cover and simmer until meat is tender, about 1 hour. Season to taste with salt, pepper, and hot sauce.

Cook grits as directed on package and add desired amount of butter. To serve, place grits on each plate. Top with the grillades. Garnish with chopped green onions.

Yield: 4-6 servings

Luncheon of Seafood and Artichokes

This is a version of a favorite luncheon served in one of New Orleans' finest restaurants. Don't let the word luncheon mislead you; it is perfect for dinner served with salad, french bread and your favorite white wine.

6   whole fresh artichokes
1   Tablespoon plus 2 teaspoons lemon juice, divided
6   Tablespoons salt
    juice of one lemon
1   stick butter
1/2 pound fresh mushrooms, sliced
1   bunch green onions and tops, minced
4   Tablespoons minced parsley
1   clove garlic, minced
1   pound fresh lump crabmeat
1/2 pound boiled shrimp
    salt and pepper, to taste
    lemon wedges, for garnish

Cut tips from artichoke leaves and coat with 1 tablespoon of the lemon juice to prevent the leaves from darkening. In a large pot, place the artichokes and enough water to cover. Add 6 tablespoons salt and the juice of the whole lemon. Bring to a boil over medium-high heat and cook until tender, about 30 minutes. (To check for tenderness, pull on the leaves. If they come off easily the artichokes are ready) Drain and cool.

Remove leaves and save for garnish. Scrape off the hairy choke and discard. A grapefruit spoon is a wonderful tool to clean the bottom. Cut the bottoms into eighths and set aside.

In a large heavy skillet over medium heat, melt 2 tablespoons of the butter. Add mushrooms and 2 teaspoons lemon juice and sauté for about 5 minutes. Add the remaining butter to the skillet and sauté the green onions (reserve 1/2 cup of onions for garnish), 2 tablespoons parsley, and the garlic until soft. Carefully mix in artichoke bottoms.

Gently fold in the crab and shrimp, being careful not to break up the crab lumps. Add the remaining lemon juice. Add salt and pepper to taste. Heat thoroughly and add 1/2 cup green onions and remaining parsley.

To serve, garnish with artichoke leaves and lemon wedges.
Yield: 4-6 servings

Crawfish Etouffée

This is probably my favorite Cajun dish. It is impossible in many areas to find crawfish meat, but you can substitute langostinos, the tiny crustaceans from Chile. Look for them in the frozen seafood section of your supermarket. If not, you can also make a wonderful shrimp étouffée by using shrimp instead of crawfish.

>   1 cup finely chopped onion
>   1 cup finely chopped celery
> 1/2 cup finely chopped green onions with tops
>   4 Tablespoons chopped shallots
>   2 cloves garlic, mashed
> 1/2 cup butter
>   2 Tablespoons flour
>   2 cups chicken stock
> 1/2 cup Rotel® tomatoes*
>   salt, to taste
>   1 teaspoon freshly ground black pepper
>   dash cayenne pepper
>   1 Tablespoon worcestershire sauce
>   2 pounds crawfish meat, langostinos, or shrimp
>   cornstarch for thickening (if necessary)
>   3 cups cooked white rice

In a heavy Dutch oven over medium heat, sauté the onion, celery, green onions, shallots and garlic in the butter. Cook until the vegetables are soft but not brown. Stir in the flour and cook until light brown, stirring constantly. Gradually add the chicken stock, stirring constantly with a wooden spoon. Add the tomatoes and simmer for 10 minutes.

Add the salt, pepper, cayenne and worcestershire, to taste. This should be spicy. If the crawfish meat has been frozen, it should be rinsed lightly and drained because it is often too salty. Add crawfish to étouffée mixture and cook over low heat for 15 minutes. Serve over the cooked rice.

Yield: 6-8 servings

*Rotel is a brand name of spicy hot tomatoes with jalapeño peppers— if you cannot find this, add hot Mexican salsa with jalapeños, to taste. I often use a whole can of Rotel—for some it may be too hot, for others it may be perfect.

Seafood Stuffed Eggplant

Every summer our garden produces an abundance of eggplants. This is one of my favorite eggplant recipes.

    1   large eggplant (1¹/2 to 2 pounds)
    1   quart salted water
    2   Tablespoons butter
 ¹/4   cup water
    1   medium onion, chopped
    2   Tablespoons chopped celery
    1   clove garlic
 ¹/2   teaspoon cayenne pepper
    1   Tablespoon oil
    2   slices bread, soaked in ¹/2 cup milk
        pinch oregano
        pinch thyme
        salt to taste
    1   egg, beaten
    4   Tablespoons cracker crumbs
 ¹/2   pound cooked crabmeat or chopped shrimp

Cut eggplant in half lengthwise. To make eggplant shell, start cutting around the edge with paring knife and scoop out all the pulp, being careful not to break the shell. Place eggplant shell in a large saucepan. Cover with quart of salted water. Cover and cook for 10 minutes. Drain, butter the skin and place in shallow baking dish. Cut the eggplant pulp into small pieces. Place in a saucepan with water and butter and cook over a low heat 15 minutes or until tender. Stir occasionally. Uncover and cook out the moisture, about 5 minutes.

Preheat oven to 350°.

In another small pan over medium heat, cook onion, celery, garlic, and cayenne in oil until tender, about 5 minutes, stirring constantly. Add soaked bread, cook and stir until glossy. Add the cooked eggplant. Season with oregano, thyme and salt. Stir well and set aside to cool. When cool add the beaten egg, 2 Tablespoons of the cracker crumbs, and the seafood. Season again if needed.

Spoon the mixture into shells and sprinkle with remaining cracker crumbs. Bake 20 minutes. The flavor will improve if stuffed eggplant is chilled several hours before baking.

Yield: 4 servings

Shrimp-and-Ham Jambalaya

Jambalaya is so versatile that almost anything can be used in it. This recipe is shown on the front cover with a different serving suggestion.

V. good (handwritten)

2 cups water
1 teaspoon salt
1 cup short-grain white rice
2 pounds medium raw shrimp
6 Tablespoons butter
1 1/2 cups finely chopped onions
2 Tablespoons finely chopped garlic
1 16-ounce can Italian plum tomatoes, chopped
3 Tablespoons tomato paste
1/2 cup chopped celery
1/4 cup finely chopped green pepper
1 Tablespoon finely chopped parsley
3/4 teaspoon powdered cloves
1/2 teaspoon dried thyme
1/2 teaspoon ground red hot pepper — *cayenne* ≈ 1/4 (handwritten)
1/4 teaspoon freshly ground black pepper
1 teaspoon salt
1 pound lean smoked ham, cut into 1/2-inch cubes

Place water, salt and rice in a medium saucepan. Bring to a boil, then lower heat, cover and simmer for 20 minutes without stirring, or until rice has absorbed liquid. Fluff the rice with a fork, cover, and set aside. Cook the shrimp as directed on page 8. Shell the shrimp and set aside.

Melt butter over moderate heat in heavy casserole. Add onions and garlic and cook for about 5 minutes, or until they are soft but not brown. Add tomatoes and tomato paste and stir over moderate heat for 5 minutes. Add celery, green pepper, parsley, cloves, thyme, red pepper, black pepper, and salt. Stirring frequently, cook uncovered over medium heat until the vegetables are tender and the mixture is thick enough to hold its shape lightly in the spoon.

Add the ham and cook for 5 minutes, stirring frequently. Stir in the shrimp and, when they are heated, add the rice. Stir over moderate heat until the mixture is hot. Taste for seasoning.

Yield: 8 servings

Shrimp Rémoulade

This cold shrimp salad makes a nice first course.

- ¹/₄ cup Creole mustard or spicy brown mustard
- 2 Tablespoons paprika
- 1 teaspoon ground red pepper
- 4 teaspoons salt
- ¹/₂ cup tarragon vinegar
- 1¹/₃ cups olive oil
- 1¹/₂ cups chopped green onions, including green tops
- ¹/₂ cups very finely chopped celery
- ¹/₂ cup coarsely chopped fresh parsley
- 2-3 pounds medium-sized cooked, deveined shrimp
- 1 large head iceberg lettuce, trimmed, quartered and cut into ¹/₄ inch shreds

Combine the mustard, paprika, red pepper, and salt in a deep bowl and stir with a wire whisk until all the ingredients are combined. Beat in the vinegar. Whisking constantly, pour in the oil in a slow, thin stream and continue to beat until the sauce is smooth and thick. Add the green onions, celery, and parsley and mix well. Cover the bowl tightly and let the sauce rest at room temperature for at least 4 hours before serving.

Just before serving; mound the shredded lettuce attractively on chilled individual serving plates and arrange the shrimp on top. Spoon the remoulade sauce over the shrimp and serve.

Yield: 6-8 first course or 4 main dish servings

Pan Barbecued Shrimp

This casual dish will be a favorite of shrimp lovers. Serve with chunks of French bread to soak up the delicious sauce.

2 pounds large uncooked, unpeeled shrimp
1 Tablespoon fresh minced parsley
$^1/_2$ cup unsalted butter
3 Tablespoons olive oil
1 teaspoon paprika
1 Tablespoon worcestershire sauce
1 Tablespoon fresh lemon juice
$^1/_2$ lemon, thinly sliced
1 teaspoon ground red pepper
$^3/_4$ teaspoon Liquid Smoke®
$^1/_2$ teaspoon dried oregano
$^1/_4$ teaspoon hot sauce
$^1/_2$ teaspoon salt
$^1/_2$ teaspoon freshly ground black pepper

Wash shrimp and slit down the back so that they will be easy to peel. You may peel before cooking, but traditionally the shrimp are cooked in the barbecue sauce in the shell. Combine remaining ingredients in a saucepan; simmer for 10 minutes. Pour over shrimp and mix thoroughly. Cover and refrigerate at least 2-3 hours, stirring occasionally.

Preheat oven to 300°. Place shrimp and sauce in a shallow pan or black iron skillet. Bake shrimp, turning frequently until they just turn pink, about 15-20 minutes. Do not overbake. Shrimp should be tender.

Yield: 4-6 servings

Shrimp Creole   tasty

Serve this delicious creole on a bed of fluffy rice.

4 Tablespoons flour
4 Tablespoons oil or bacon drippings
1 1/2 cups chopped white onions
1 bunch green onions, chopped
1 cup chopped celery, including some of the leaves
1 large green pepper, chopped
2 cloves garlic, minced
1 6-ounce can tomato paste
1 16-ounce can plum tomatoes with liquid, chopped
1 8-ounce can tomato sauce
1 cup water
1 1/2 teaspoons salt, or to taste
1 teaspoon freshly ground black pepper
1/4 1/2 teaspoon cayenne
  dash hot sauce
2 bay leaves
2 teaspoons worcestershire sauce
1 Tablespoon fresh lemon juice
3-4 pounds raw shrimp, peeled and deveined
1 cup short-grain white rice
2 cups water
1 teaspoon salt
1/2 cup fresh parsley, for garnish

40 mins
Make a dark roux with the flour and oil, following the directions on page 7. Add the onions, green onions, celery, green pepper, and garlic. Cook slowly until the vegetables are soft but not brown. Add the tomato paste, tomatoes, tomato sauce, water, salt, pepper, cayenne, hot sauce, bay leaves, worcestershire and lemon juice. Simmer very slowly for 1 hour, covered.

While the creole cooks, make the rice by placing the rice, water and salt in a medium saucepan. Bring to a boil. Reduce heat, cover and simmer for 20 minutes or until rice has absorbed liquid. Fluff the rice with a fork, cover and set aside.

Add shrimp to creole and cook for 3-5 minutes, or just until done. To serve, spoon the creole over the rice and garnish with parsley.

Yield: 8-10 servings

Vegetables & Side Dishes

Green Beans Horseradish

Spicy and interesting—these beans are excellent served hot or cold. The traditional way to cook green beans in the South has been to cook them all morning long. I prefer to use fresh or frozen beans and cook just until tender.

1- 1¹/₂ pounds fresh green beans
           several bits of ham or bacon, as flavoring
1   large onion, sliced
1   cup mayonnaise
2   hard boiled eggs, peeled and chopped
1   Tablespoon horseradish
1   teaspoon worcestershire sauce
     salt and freshly ground black pepper, to taste
     garlic powder, to taste
     celery seed to taste
3   Tablespoons minced parsley
     juice of 1 lemon

   In a large saucepan over medium heat, cook beans with meat and sliced onions, until beans reach desired tenderness. If you use raw pork, make sure that the pork is done. In a medium mixing bowl, blend mayonnaise with eggs, horseradish, worcestershire sauce, salt, pepper, garlic powder, celery seed, parsley and lemon juice. Drain beans and spoon mayonnaise mixture over the beans.
   Yield: 6 servings

Louisiana Red Beans and Rice

Red beans and rice is a hearty, satisfying, unpretentious meal that is popular in south Louisiana. It is traditionally eaten on Mondays, made with Sunday's leftover ham.

6	cups water
1	pound dried red kidney beans
4	Tablespoons butter
1	cup finely chopped green onions, including tops
1/2	cup finely chopped onions
1	rib celery, chopped
1	teaspoon finely chopped garlic
1	ham bone with ham attached or
	2-pounds smoked ham hocks
1	pound hot smoked sausage, optional
1	teaspoon salt
1	bay leaf
1/2	teaspoon freshly ground pepper
	dash red pepper, optional
	cumin, to taste
3	cups cooked white rice
	additional chopped green onions, for garnish

In a large saucepan over high heat, bring 6 cups water to a boil. Add beans and boil briskly for 2 minutes. Turn off heat and let beans soak for 1 hour.

In a heavy casserole over medium heat, melt butter and cook green onions, white onions, celery, and garlic until soft but not brown. Stir in beans and liquid, the ham bone or ham hocks, sausage and the seasonings. Bring to boil over high heat, then reduce heat and simmer, partially covered, for 3 hours or until beans are very soft. If the beans seem dry, add more hot water a few tablespoons at a time. Stir frequently.

Remove ham bones, cut meat from the bone and return meat to beans. Remove the bay leaf.

Serve red beans with cooked white rice. To garnish, sprinkle chopped green onions over the top.

Yield: 4-6 servings.

Garden District Broccoli

The red wine, cheese, tomatoes, and olives give this vegetable dish an unusual flavor.

  1 large bunch broccoli
  1 Tablespoon olive oil
  1 large white onion, thinly sliced
  2 tomatoes, thinly sliced, or one 16-ounce can tomato wedges
  ¹/₂ cup sliced black olives
  1 anchovy fillet cut into small pieces
  ¹/₂ cup grated Romano cheese
  1 cup dry red wine

Wash broccoli and cut the stalks lengthwise into thin pieces. In a heavy skillet over medium heat, warm the olive oil and add a layer of sliced onion, tomato, black olives, and anchovy. Top with a layer of the broccoli and sprinkle with Romano cheese. Repeat the process until all is used up, reserving a few pieces of anchovy. Pour in the red wine.

Cover the skillet and cook over low heat for 10-15 minutes or until broccoli is just tender. Garnish with the remaining pieces of anchovy.

Yield: 4-6 servings

Artichokes Creole Style

This artichoke casserole makes a nice side dish to any meal.

  ¹/₂ cup chopped onion
  3 Tablespoons finely chopped green onion
  ¹/₂ cup butter
  1 35-ounce can Italian plum tomatoes, drained
  1 14-ounce can artichoke hearts, drained
  1 teaspoon fresh basil or ¹/₂ teaspoon dried basil
  1 Tablespoon sugar
      salt and pepper, to taste
  ¹/₂ cup freshly grated Parmesan cheese

Preheat oven to 325°.

In a medium skillet over medium heat, sauté onion and green onions in butter until tender. Add tomatoes, artichoke hearts, basil, sugar, salt and pepper. Stir gently over medium heat until mixture bubbles. Taste for seasoning. Pour into greased baking dish and cover with Parmesan cheese.

Bake at 325° for 20 minutes or until bubbling hot and browned on top.

Yield: 4 servings.

Southern Fried Okra

Many people think they won't like okra, but it is delicious prepared in this fashion.

1¹/₂ pounds okra, washed, drained, and thinly sliced
2 quarts salted water
1 ¹/₂ cups cornmeal seasoned with salt and pepper
1 cup vegetable oil

Soak okra in salted water for 30 minutes. Drain, rinse, and dry. Shake okra in a paper or plastic bag with the seasoned cornmeal. In a large skillet or deep fryer, bring vegetable oil to frying temperature. Fry okra in hot oil until golden brown. Drain on paper towels.
Yield: 4-6 servings

Spiced Stewed Okra

This is another favorite okra dish.

1¹/₂ pounds fresh okra
3 cups water
3 large firm ripe tomatoes
¹/₂ pound sliced bacon, cut crosswise into halves
1 cup chopped white onions
1 cup coarsely chopped green peppers
3 dried hot red chilies, each about 2-inches long, washed, stemmed, seeded and coarsely crumbled
1 teaspoon salt

Wash okra under cold running water. Scrape the skin lightly to remove surface fuzz. Cut off stems and slice pods into ¹/₂-inch rounds.

In a medium saucepan over high heat, bring 3 cups water to a full boil. Drop tomatoes into boiling water for 15 seconds. Remove and run under cold water to loosen the skins. Peel the tomatoes, cut each in half and squeeze gently to remove seeds and juice. Discard seeds and juice. Coarsely chop the pulp.

In a medium skillet over medium heat, fry the bacon pieces until they are crisp and brown. Drain on paper towel.

Pour off all but ¹/₄ cup of the bacon fat and add onions and green peppers to skillet. Stirring frequently, cook for about 5 minutes until the vegetables are soft but not brown.

Add the okra and still stirring occasionally, cook over medium heat for 15 minutes, or until okra is tender. Add tomatoes, chilies, and salt; reduce the heat to low and simmer, tightly covered, for 10 minutes.

Taste and adjust seasoning if necessary. To serve, place in a pretty serving bowl and garnish with the cooked bacon.
Yield: 6 servings

Spinach Madeline

This delightful spinach casserole also makes a wonderful hot dip.

> 2   10-ounce packages frozen chopped spinach
> 4   Tablespoons butter
> 2   Tablespoons flour
> 2   Tablespoons chopped onion
> 1   clove garlic, finely minced
> 1/2 cup reserved liquid from spinach
> 1/2 cup evaporated milk or light cream
>   black pepper, to taste
> 3/4 teaspoon celery seed
> 8   ounces jalapeño pepper cheese, grated
> 1   teaspoon worcestershire sauce
>   red pepper, to taste
>   cornbread stuffing mix or cracker crumbs

Preheat oven to 350°.

Thaw spinach in microwave oven but do not fully cook. Drain, reserving 1/2 cup of spinach juice for the sauce.

In heavy saucepan over low heat, melt the butter. Add flour stirring for 2-3 minutes but do not brown. Add the onion and garlic, and cook until soft but do not brown. Add the spinach liquid and milk or cream, stirring to avoid lumps. Add the pepper, celery seed, cheese, worcestershire sauce and red pepper. Stir until the cheese has melted. Combine with the spinach.

Pour into a buttered casserole dish, and cover with stuffing mix or cracker crumbs. (At this point the casserole can be refrigerated.) Bake at 350° until hot and bubbling, about 15-20 minutes.

Yield: 6 servings

Cajun Dirty Rice

This hearty side dish is good with many things. It is definitely best when made the day before.

1	package chicken necks or chicken parts (for stock)
6	cups water
	salt, to taste
	pepper, to taste
1	rib celery, cut into chunks
1	bay leaf
1/2	pound chicken gizzards
1/2	pound chicken livers
3/4	pound ground beef
2	cups raw rice
1/2	cup butter
1 1/2	cups minced green onions
2	onions, chopped
6	large ribs celery, finely chopped
1	large green pepper, chopped
2	cloves garlic, minced
1/2	cup fresh parsley, minced
1	teaspoon salt
1/2	teaspoon freshly ground black pepper
1/4	teaspoon cayenne pepper
1/2	teaspoon dried thyme or 1 teaspoon fresh

To make the stock, in a large saucepan place chicken necks in 6 cups water seasoned with salt, pepper, celery and bay leaf. Bring to a boil, then reduced heat and simmer for 1-2 hours. Strain broth and set aside 2½ cups. In remaining broth, boil the gizzards until tender. Set aside. In the same broth, cook the chicken livers (they will cook faster than the gizzards). Cool the gizzards and livers slightly and mince.

In a small skillet, brown the ground beef until no longer pink. Drain off fat and set aside.

In a large saucepan, bring 2½ cups of the reserved broth and 2 cups rice to a boil. Lower heat, cover, and cook for about 20 minutes or until most of the liquid is absorbed by the rice.

In a large skillet over medium heat, melt ½ cup butter. Add the green onions, white onions, celery, green pepper, garlic and parsley and sauté vegetables until soft but not brown.

Mix the rice, giblets and ground beef into the sautéed vegetables. Cook and stir, adding extra broth to moisten the mixture as necessary. Season with salt, pepper, cayenne, and thyme.

Continue cooking and stirring over a very low heat for 20 minutes or so. Place in a baking dish and reheat when ready to serve.

Yield: 12 servings.

Golden Garlic Cheese Grits

For many people in Louisiana, breakfast is just not breakfast without grits. Try this dressed up version for your next brunch. It can be made the day before.

        1   cup grits, uncooked
      ¹/2   cup butter
        8   ounces garlic-flavored cheese (if you cannot find
            this, use a processed cheddar cheese and 1 clove
            garlic minced very fine)
            freshly ground black pepper to taste
            cayenne pepper to taste
        2   Tablespoons worcestershire sauce
        2   eggs, separated
            paprika, to taste

Preheat oven to 350°.

Cook grits in salted water as directed on package. When cooked, add the butter, cheese, pepper, cayenne, and worcestershire sauce. Stir until the butter and cheese have melted. Add the egg yolks and stir well. In a medium mixing bowl, using an electric mixer, stiffly beat the two egg whites. Fold into grits mixture.

Pour into a greased casserole, and sprinkle with paprika. Bake at 350° for 30 minutes or until golden brown.

Yield: 8-10 servings

Festive Hot Fruit Casserole

Banana liqueur is the secret ingredient in this delicious hot fruit casserole. It has been a brunch favorite of many of my students.

1	28-ounce can peach slices
1	15-ounce can pineapple chunks
1	15-ounce can apricot halves
1	box dried figs, cooked according to package directions
4	sliced bananas
	fresh lemon juice
3	dozen almond macaroon cookies, coarsely crushed
1	can slivered almonds
	brown sugar, to taste
	butter, to taste
1/4	cup banana liqueur or Cointreau®

Preheat oven to 300°.

Drain the canned fruits and pat dry with paper towels. Sprinkle banana slices with lemon juice. Mix all of the fruits together and put half the fruit mixture in a buttered 2-quart casserole. Sprinkle with 1/2 of the macaroon crumbs and 1/2 of the almonds. Sprinkle with brown sugar and dot with butter. Repeat the layers. Pour the banana liqueur over the top. Bake at 300° for 20-30 minutes or until hot and bubbly.

Yield: 12 servings

Chilled Herbed Whole Tomatoes

This could be the basis of a beautiful salad plate. Just add chilled asparagus and a chicken or seafood salad. Wonderful in the summer when your garden is producing fresh tomatoes.

       6 *whole ripe tomatoes*
       4 *cups water*
     $^2/_3$ *cup vegetable or olive oil*
     $^1/_4$ *cup red wine vinegar*
       1 *clove minced garlic*
     $^1/_4$ *cup chopped parsley*
     $^1/_4$ *cup sliced green onions, including tops*
       1 *teaspoon salt*
     $^1/_4$ *teaspoon freshly ground black pepper*
     $^1/_2$ *teaspoon dried thyme or 1 teaspoon fresh thyme*
     $^1/_2$ *teaspoon dried basil or 1 teaspoon fresh basil*
          minced green onions and parsley, for garnish

In a large saucepan over high heat, bring water to a full boil. Drop tomatoes into boiling water for a few seconds to make skin removal easy. Remove tomatoes and peel.

In a medium glass or plastic mixing bowl, combine the remaining ingredients. Add tomatoes and marinate for several hours or overnight.

To serve, arrange the tomatoes on a serving platter. Spoon a small amount of marinade over each tomato and sprinkle with minced green onions and parsley.

Yield: 6 servings

Purple Passion Tomatoes

This is another favorite tomato dish of mine.

2   large purple onions, cut into slices
6   large firm ripe tomatoes, peeled and quartered
1   green pepper, cut into strips
³/4 cup cider vinegar
¹/4 cup water
1¹/2 teaspoons celery seed
1¹/2 teaspoons mustard seed
¹/2 teaspoon salt
2   Tablespoons sugar
¹/2 teaspoon or more of freshly grated black pepper

Place onions, tomatoes, and green pepper in bowl. Place vinegar, water, celery seed, mustard seed, salt, sugar, and pepper in a saucepan and bring to a boil. Boil for 1 minute. While still hot, pour over vegetables. Chill.
Yield: 6 servings

Leek Salad

The spicy dressing for this salad is good on other salads as well.

8   leeks
¹/2 cup cooking liquid from the leeks
¹/2 cup sour cream
¹/2 cup cider vinegar
¹/2 teaspoon Creole mustard or spicy brown mustard
1   teaspoon horseradish
¹/2 teaspoon salt
¹/4 teaspoon hot pepper sauce

Clean leeks by removing roots and outside leaves. Trim leaves until they are about 6-7 inches long. Wash well to get rid of sand. Cut leeks in half.

In a medium saucepan over medium heat, cook leeks in water until just tender, 10-15 minutes. Drain leeks, reserving cooking water. Refrigerate until well chilled.

In a medium mixing bowl, combine half cup of leek cooking water, sour cream, vinegar, mustard, horseradish, salt and hot sauce. Beat the dressing with a whisk.

To serve, pour dressing over leeks.
Yield: 4 servings

Eggs & Egg Sauces

Shrimp and Mushrooms on Deviled Eggs

This egg dish combines shrimp and mushrooms. It is perfect for a luncheon.

$^1/_2$ pound fresh mushrooms sautéed in butter
8 eggs, deviled (use your favorite recipe)
1 pound shelled cooked shrimp
$^1/_4$ cup butter
$^1/_4$ cup flour
$1^1/_2$ cups milk
$1^1/_2$ cups grated cheddar cheese
dash sherry
dash cayenne pepper
salt and pepper, to taste
$^1/_2$ teaspoon worcestershire sauce

Preheat oven to 350°.

Cover the bottom of a 2-quart casserole with the sautéed mushrooms. Top with your favorite deviled eggs. Cover these with the shrimp.

In a medium saucepan over medium heat, melt the butter until bubbling. Stir in flour and cook 3-5 minutes. Add milk gradually, stirring until smooth. Stir in 1 cup of the cheese and stir until melted. Add the sherry, cayenne, salt, pepper, and worcestershire. Taste for seasoning.

Pour cheese sauce over the mushrooms, eggs, and shrimp. Cover with remaining cheese. (At this point you may refrigerate the casserole. Remove it from refrigerator 30 minutes before cooking.) Bake at 350° for approximately 30 minutes.

Yield: 4 servings.

Eggs Houssarde

The wonderful wine sauce used in this egg dish is also delicious as a filling for crepes or served over beef.

Marchands de Vin Sauce

- 1/4 cup butter
- 1/3 cup minced mushrooms
- 1/2 cup minced green onions
- 1/2 cup minced onion
- 2-3 cloves garlic, minced
- 1/2 cup minced ham
- 2 Tablespoons flour
  black pepper to taste
  cayenne pepper to taste
- 3/4 cup beef stock
- 1/2 cup claret wine
  salt, to taste

- 6 slices Canadian bacon
- 6 Holland Rusks or toasted English muffins
- 6 poached eggs, cooked as directed below
- 1 recipe Hollandaise Sauce, page 49
  paprika, for garnish
  fresh parsley, for garnish

In a medium skillet over medium heat, melt the butter. Add the mushrooms, green onions, onion, and garlic and sauté until the vegetables are soft. Add ham and cook for one minute. Stir in flour, pepper, and cayenne. Brown mixture lightly about 10 minutes, stirring constantly. Blend in beef stock and wine. Add salt if necessary. Cover and simmer 15 minutes over low heat, stirring occasionally. May be refrigerated until needed.

Broil the Canadian bacon until hot. Place one piece on each Holland rusk or toasted English muffin. Cover with the Marchands de Vin Sauce. Top each with a poached egg. Spoon Hollandaise sauce over the eggs. Garnish with paprika and fresh parsley.

Yield: 6 servings

How to Poach An Egg: Use a shallow saucepan or skillet. Add enough water to cover the eggs. Add salt and 1 tablespoon vinegar and bring just to a boil. (The vinegar helps to coagulate the eggs). Break each egg into a saucer and slip the eggs one at a time into the boiling water. Cover and cook 2-3 minutes until eggs are the desired doneness. Never put eggs into rapidly boiling water, but let them simmer gently until done.

Eggs Nouvelle Orleans

Poached eggs and crabmeat with Brandied Cream Sauce makes a great combination.

Brandied Cream Sauce:
- 3 Tablespoons butter
- 2 Tablespoons finely chopped onion
- 3 Tablespoons flour
- 1¹/₂ cups milk
- 2 Tablespoons brandy
- 1 teaspoon fresh lemon juice
- ¹/₈ Tablespoon cayenne
- 1 teaspoon salt

In a heavy saucepan over medium heat, melt the butter. Add onions and cook until they are soft but not brown. Add flour and cook 2 minutes, stirring constantly. Whisk in milk and cook until sauce thickens and is smooth.

In a small pan, warm the brandy and ignite. When the flame subsides add to the sauce with the lemon juice, cayenne, and salt. Taste for seasoning. Keep warm while you prepare the crabmeat and eggs.

- 8 Tablespoons butter cut into ¹/₂ inch pieces
- 1 pound fresh crabmeat, all shell removed
- ¹/₂ teaspoon salt
- ¹/₂ teaspoon cayenne
- 8 eggs
- 1-2 Tablespoons vinegar
- ¹/₂ teaspoon paprika

In a large skillet over medium heat, melt the butter and add crabmeat, salt and cayenne to taste. Sauté the crabmeat about 6 minutes over medium heat.

Poach eggs in water with 1-2 Tablespoons vinegar (see directions on page 45). Divide sautéed crabmeat among 4 baking ramekins and cover each portion with 2 poached eggs. Top with brandied cream sauce. Sprinkle with paprika.

Serve with toast or garlic bread.

Yield: 4 servings

Eggs Sardou

1 recipe Creamed Spinach, below
1 can artichoke bottoms
2 cups salted water
12 poached eggs
1 recipe Hollandaise Sauce , page 49
    paprika, to taste

Make creamed spinach as directed in the recipe below. Drain artichoke bottoms. In a large saucepan, warm the artichokes in salted water. To assemble, place 2 artichoke bottoms on each plate, fill with creamed spinach, place one poached egg on each and top with generous amount of Hollandaise. Sprinkle with paprika.
Yield: 6 servings

Creamed Spinach

I have used this spinach in many different ways. For a lovely luncheon or brunch dish, add crabmeat or shrimp and mushrooms and serve in a buttered casserole.

2   10-ounce packages frozen chopped spinach
5   Tablespoons butter, divided
1   medium onion, chopped
4   Tablespoons flour
2   cups milk
3   egg yolks
    salt and pepper, to taste
    dash nutmeg
1   cup cream
1/4 cup Parmesan cheese

Cook spinach according to package directions. Drain well and set aside.

In a large saucepan, melt 1 tablespoon butter. Add onions and sauté until soft but not brown. Add 4 tablespoons of butter and melt until foaming. Add flour and cook over low heat for 3 minutes. Add the milk gradually, beating with a wire whisk to avoid lumps. Cook over low heat, stirring with a wooden spoon until smooth.

In a small mixing bowl, beat the egg yolks slightly. Spoon some of the hot sauce into egg yolks and beat with a fork. Add egg mixture to the white sauce, beating constantly. Add the salt, pepper, and nutmeg. Cook slowly for a few minutes until sauce thickens further.

Add the cream and Parmesan cheese. Add the drained spinach. Proceed with the Eggs Sardou recipe above, or pour into a buttered casserole and serve warm.
Yield: 4-6 servings

Bearnaise Sauce

This is a versatile sauce that all cooks should know how to make.

- $^1/_3$ cup dry white wine
- $^1/_3$ cup tarragon vinegar
- $^1/_4$ cup finely chopped green onions and some tops
- 1   teaspoon dried tarragon or 2 teaspoons fresh
- 2   sprigs fresh parsley
- $^1/_4$ teaspoon whole black peppercorns
- 1   Tablespoon water
- 2   Tablespoons fresh lemon juice
- 4   egg yolks
- 2   Tablespoons butter, melted
- $^1/_4$ teaspoon cayenne

In a small non-aluminum saucepan, bring the wine, vinegar, onions, tarragon, parsley, and peppercorns to a boil. Cook until it is reduced to about 2 tablespoons. Strain the liquid and press the solids to get as much of the flavor from them as you can. Add the water and lemon juice to the reduced wine mixture and heat to a simmer.

Place a glass mixing bowl into a skillet of boiling water (I prefer this to a double boiler). Whisk the egg yolks in the mixing bowl until thick and lemon-colored. Add the above liquid a tablespoon at a time and whisk after each. The mixture should be thick and almost doubled in size. Dribble in butter, whisking constantly until the mixture forms a slowly dissolving ribbon when drawn across itself. Whisk in cayenne.

Hint: The sauce thickens considerably within the first few minutes after it is removed from the heat. Don't try to make a Hollandaise or Bearnaise sauce too thick while it is over the heat or you may end up with scrambled eggs floating in butter.

Hollandaise Sauce

Follow the directions carefully and you will have perfect Hollandaise every time. Do not use an aluminum pot or you may end up with a green sauce.

    1/2   cup butter
  1 1/2   Tablespoons lemon juice, or less to taste
      3   egg yolks
      4   Tablespoons boiling water
          dash cayenne pepper
    1/4   teaspoon salt

You will need a wire whisk and a glass double boiler. This substitution for a glass double boiler works better than the real thing, so I suggest you use it: a medium glass mixing bowl in a skillet that is partially full of water. The butter may be melted in a container in the skillet, the lemon juice warmed, and the boiling water to be used in the sauce is accessible from the skillet.

Melt the butter slowly and keep warm. Heat the lemon juice. Place 3 egg yolks in a glass mixing bowl in a skillet of hot water. The water should not be too hot or the eggs will scramble.

Beat the 3 egg yolks with a wire whisk until they begin to thicken. Add 1 tablespoon boiling water. Beat until eggs begin to thicken. Repeat until you have added 3 *more* Tablespoons water. Beat in the warm lemon juice.

Beat sauce well with wire whisk. Beat constantly while *slowly* adding the melted butter and 1/4 teaspoon salt and dash cayenne.

Beat until the sauce is almost thick enough. The sauce should form a slowly dissolving ribbon when sauce is drawn across the surface. It will thicken considerably in the first minute after removing from the heat. Do not overcook.

Hint: Hollandaise sauce may be held for several hours in a wide mouth thermos bottle. If the sauce should break or begin to curdle, beat in 1 or 2 Tablespoons of cream.

Breads

French Market Doughnuts

Try these puffy sugar-covered beignets with piping hot café au lait.

  1 *cup milk*
  ¹/4 *cup sugar*
  ³/4 *teaspoon salt*
  ¹/2 *teaspoon freshly grated nutmeg*
  2 *Tablespoons lukewarm water*
  1 *package active dry yeast*
  2 *Tablespoons vegetable oil*
  1 *egg*
 3¹/2 *cups sifted all-purpose flour*
   confectioners sugar, for garnish

In a medium saucepan over medium-high heat, scald the milk. Add sugar, salt, and nutmeg. Cool to lukewarm.

Place 2 tablespoons warm water in a large mixing bowl. Sprinkle yeast into warm water, stirring until yeast is dissolved.

Add the oil, egg, and dissolved yeast to the lukewarm milk mixture, blending with a spoon. Add the flour gradually, beating well. The dough will be very soft. Cover with plastic wrap, then a clean towel, and let rise in a warm place until doubled in size.

Turn dough onto a well-floured surface; knead gently. Roll into an 18 by 12-inch rectangle; cut into 36 rectangles 3 x 2-inches. Cover with a towel and let rise for ¹/2 hour.

Fry doughnuts 2 at a time in deep fat (375°) until golden brown. Drain on paper towels. Shake in a brown bag with confectioners sugar. Serve hot.

Yield: 36 doughnuts

Popover Pancake

A cross between an omelet and a pancake. Wonderful served with fresh strawberries or peaches, or filled with a savory stuffing. This simple dish is a favorite at our house.

3 eggs
1/2 teaspoon salt
1/2 cup sifted flour
1/2 cup milk
    dash freshly grated nutmeg
6 Tablespoons butter
    juice of 1/2 lemon
    confectioners sugar
    your favorite jam, syrup, jelly, or fresh fruit

Preheat oven to 450°.

Combine eggs, salt, flour, milk, and nutmeg in a medium mixing bowl. Beat with an electric mixer at medium speed until thoroughly blended. Grease the bottom and sides of a cold 8-inch iron skillet with 3 Tablespoons of butter. Pour in the batter and bake in the hot oven for 15 to 20 minutes or until the crust is golden brown.

Melt the remaining 3 Tablespoons of butter with the lemon juice. When the pancake comes out of the oven pour the lemon butter over the pancake and sprinkle with the confectioners sugar. Serve with your favorite topping.

Yield: 4 servings

Joem Hough

Cornbread Sticks

You will need a special iron breadstick pan if you want to make this cornbread in the traditional corn-shaped sticks.

2 cups buttermilk
$^1/_2$ teaspoon baking soda
$1^1/_2$ cups cornmeal
$^3/_4$ cup flour
3 Tablespoons sugar
$1^1/_2$ teaspoons salt
2 teaspoons baking powder
2 eggs, beaten
8 Tablespoons oil

Preheat oven to 450°. Grease cornbread pan and set aside.
Mix the buttermilk and soda and let stand for 20 minutes.
Combine the corn meal, flour, sugar, salt, and baking powder. Add the eggs, oil, and the buttermilk mixture. Mix just until moistened.
Heat greased cornbread pan in hot oven until the oil sizzles. Fill pan half full with batter. Bake for 15 minutes or until a beautiful golden brown.
Yield: 22 sticks

Jean Hough

Sweet Potato Bread

This sweet potato bread is full of sugar and spice and everything nice.

     1 stick butter
    ¹/₂ cup yogurt
    ¹/₂ cup honey
     1 teaspoon cinnamon
   1¹/₂ cups chopped pecans, divided
     2 cups grated raw sweet potatoes
   3¹/₂ cups flour
     3 cups sugar
     2 teaspoons baking soda
     2 teaspoons salt
     1 teaspoon nutmeg
     1 teaspoon cinnamon
     1 cup cooking oil
    ³/₄ cup water
     4 eggs, beaten

Preheat oven to 350°.

Combine butter, yogurt, honey, and cinnamon in a saucepan and boil 1 minute. Stir in 1 cup of pecans. Allow this mixture to cool.

Mix the remaining pecans with sweet potatoes.

In a large mixing bowl blend the flour, sugar, baking soda, salt, nutmeg, and cinnamon.

In a small bowl mix the oil, water, and eggs. Add sweet potatoes and pecans to the flour mixture. Pour in the liquid mixture and blend just to moisten.

Line two 9x5-inch loaf pans with greased foil or parchment paper. Place 1 cup of batter in each pan. Top each with ¹/₂ cup of cooled butter and honey mixture, cover with another cup of batter, then another ¹/₂ cup of butter mixture. Finish with remaining batter. Bake for 65-75 minutes until bread cracks and the center is dry.

Cool 15 minutes. Remove from pan and store wrapped in foil or plastic wrap. Best sliced the following day.

Yield: 2 loaves.

Desserts

Fresh Strawberry Pie

We look forward to the time when strawberries are in season so we can make this pie. You can make a wonderful fresh peach pie using the same recipe. Just substitute peaches for the strawberries and add 1 tablespoon butter to the peach glaze after it thickens and becomes clear.

> 2 pints fresh strawberries
> ³/4 cup water
> 1 Tablespoon fresh lemon juice
> 3 Tablespoons cornstarch
> 1 cup sugar
> 1 9-inch baked pie shell
> 1 cup whipping cream
> 1 teaspoon vanilla
> 1 Tablespoon confectioners' sugar

Wash and hull the strawberries. Measure 1 cup of berries for the glaze and mash them or puree in blender. Pour into a medium saucepan. Add water and lemon juice.

Over medium heat, bring the fruit mixture to a simmer and cook for 1-2 minutes. Mix cornstarch with sugar and add to the berries. Cook until the mixture thickens and becomes clear. Cool slightly.

Put the remaining berries (they may be sliced or left whole) into the baked shell. Pour the strawberry sauce over the berries and chill.

Using an electric mixer, beat the whipping cream until it forms stiff peaks. Flavor with the vanilla and sugar. See about Whipped Cream on page 55.

Yield: 8 servings

New Orleans Coffee Bavarian Cream

Buy some delicious mocha coffee bean candies for garnish.

1 envelope Knox® gelatine
2 Tablespoons cold water
2 Tablespoons cold, very strong New Orleans coffee
2 Tablespoons Coffee Amaretto
4 egg yolks
1/2 cup sugar
1 cup milk, scalded
1 cup heavy cream, stiffly-whipped

Soften gelatine in a mixture of the cold water, coffee, and Amaretto. Beat the egg yolks with the sugar until smooth and creamy. Combine with the scalded milk and cook over low heat, stirring constantly, until smooth and thick—about 10 minutes.

Add softened gelatine and continue to stir until the gelatine is completely dissolved. Cool, stirring from time to time to prevent a crust from forming. Fold in the stiffly-whipped cream.

Serve in stemmed glasses or small bowls and add a dash of Coffee Amaretto for garnish.

Yield: 4-6 servings

About Whipped Cream: When whipping cream, place a piece of waxed paper with a slit in it over the beaters. This prevents the splattering of cream. When the cream is stiff enough to have some body, you can remove the paper and continue to whip without getting cream on your clothing. Remember to chill the mixing bowl and beaters. Do not over whip.

Ultra-pasteurized creams have a long shelf life, but I prefer the whipping qualities and the flavor of whipping cream that is labeled *pasteurized* instead of *ultra-pasteurized.* If a recipe calls for adding flavoring or sugar, do this when the cream forms very soft peaks. Continue beating to desired consistency.

Bread Pudding with Whiskey Sauce

Don't let the humble name fool you. This traditional New Orleans dessert is rich and hearty.

   2   Tablespoons butter, softened
  12   ounce loaf day-old French or Italian-style white bread
   1   quart milk
   3   eggs
   1   cup sugar
 1/2   cup raisins
   2   Tablespoons vanilla extract
 1/2   teaspoon freshly grated nutmeg
 1/2   teaspoon cinnamon

Sauce:
   8   Tablespoons butter cut into bits
   1   cup sugar
   1   egg
 1/2   cup bourbon or brandy

Preheat oven to 350°. Butter a 13x9x2-inch baking dish and set aside.

Break bread into chunks, dropping them into a bowl. Pour milk over them. When bread has softened, crumble into small bits and let soak until all the milk is absorbed.

In a small bowl, beat 3 eggs and 1 cup of sugar with whisk or electric mixer until the mixture is smooth and thick. Stir in the raisins, vanilla extract, nutmeg and cinnamon. Pour the egg mixture over the bread crumbs and stir until all the ingredients are well-combined.

Pour the bread pudding into baking dish. Place the dish in a large shallow roasting pan set in the middle of the oven. Add water to the roasting pan to a depth of about 1 inch. Bake 1 hour or until a knife inserted in the center comes out clean.

Whiskey Sauce

Melt butter bits in top of double boiler set over hot, not boiling, water. Stir 1 cup of sugar and 1 egg together in a small bowl and add the mixture to the butter. Stir for 2 to 3 minutes, until the sugar dissolves completely, or the egg will curdle. Remove the pan from the heat and let the sauce cool to room temperature before stirring in the bourbon.

Serve the bread pudding at once and pass the whiskey sauce separately.

Yield: 8-10 servings

Never Fail Flaky Pie Crust

I have had many people in my cooking classes come back and thank me for this recipe. No matter how much you handle this dough it will always be flaky and tender. The dough may be refrigerated for three days or it may be frozen until ready to use. This recipe will make 4-5 single crusts.

4^1/2   cups unsifted all-purpose flour
1   Tablespoon sugar
2   teaspoons salt
1^3/4   cups solid vegetable shortening (no substitutions)
1   large egg
1   Tablespoon white or cider vinegar
^{1}/2   cup water

Put the flour, sugar, and salt in a large bowl and mix well with a fork. Add shortening and mix with fork until ingredients are crumbly. In a small bowl, beat egg, vinegar, and the water. Combine the two mixtures, stirring with a fork until all ingredients are moistened. Divide the dough into 5 portions. Wrap each in plastic wrap and chill for at least ^{1}/2 hour.

I always roll my pie crust out between two pieces of plastic wrap. This makes the job easier by eliminating the need for extra flour, which often makes a mess. When pie crust is rolled to the desired size, peel off the top piece of the plastic wrap. Then handle the pie crust from the bottom with the remaining plastic. This is very easy to work with. Invert into pie plate and peel off plastic.

Baked Shell
Prick bottom and sides of pastry thoroughly. To keep shell flat, place parchment paper or foil over crust. Press gently into the crust. This will help prevent shrinking. Put on a rack in the center of a preheated 400° oven. Bake 10 minutes or until crust has set. Then remove foil or parchment and bake until brown for about 5-8 minutes.

Hint: Shiny metal pans reflect the heat away from the crust. For better browning of the crust use a dark metal or glass pan.

Dessert Crêpe Batter

Once you learn the art, you will make these crêpes again and again. The beauty of crêpes lies in their versatility. Fillings may be simple or elaborate. Crêpes can be made ahead of time and frozen.

$^3/_4$ cup cold milk
$^3/_4$ cup cold water
3 egg yolks
1 Tablespoon granulated sugar
$1^1/_2$ cups flour
3 Tablespoons orange liqueur, rum, or brandy
5 Tablespoons melted butter

Blend all the ingredients in an electric blender for one minute. Refrigerate for a minimum of 1 hour so that the flour particles will swell and the crêpes will be light.

Many different pans can be used for making crêpes. I prefer to use a $6^1/_2$-inch cast iron crêpe pan. Others prefer to use a non-stick skillet. You will probably have success with your favorite skillet.

The key factor to success is getting the correct heat. Heat the pan over a medium high heat. When a drop of water begins to dance on the surface, brush the pan lightly with shortening or oil. (It is not necessary to oil the pan between each crêpe.) Pour a scant $^1/_4$ cup of batter into the pan while quickly tilting the pan in all directions so that the batter will coat the bottom of the pan evenly. Pour off excess batter so that the crêpe will be paper thin. Cook until the crêpe is set and lightly browned on the bottom. Crêpes can be browned on both sides, but this is not necessary. Place crêpes in a single layer on a platter or wax paper covered countertop to cool.

Crêpes may be frozen. To freeze, stack between layers of waxed paper and then wrap in foil.

Yield: 14-16 crepes

Lemon Soufflé Crêpes

What could be more special than a lemon soufflé peeking from a crisp crêpe and topped with a delicious raspberry sauce?

  3   *Tablespoons unsalted butter*
  5   *Tablespoons flour*
$^1/_2$ *cup hot milk*
  3   *eggs, separated*
  4   *Tablespoons sugar, divided plus additional for garnish*
  3   *Tablespoons strained fresh lemon juice*
  1   *Tablespoon freshly grated lemon peel*
      pinch salt
12 *dessert crêpes*

Preheat oven to 400°.

Melt 3 Tablespoons butter in a heavy saucepan over a low heat. Stir in the flour and cook for 1 to 2 minutes. Remove from the heat and whisk in the milk. Return to the heat and cook until the sauce thickens.

In a small bowl beat the egg yolks with a fork. Add small amounts of the sauce to the eggs to temper them so they won't "scramble" when added to the white sauce. Whisk the eggs into the sauce. Add 3 Tablespoons of the sugar, the lemon juice and the lemon peel, stirring thoroughly until all the ingredients are combined.

In a separate bowl, beat the egg whites with a pinch of salt. Gradually add the remaining tablespoon of sugar and beat until the whites form stiff peaks. With a rubber spatula, carefully stir one fourth of the egg whites into the lemon mixture. When this mixture is sufficiently "lightened" carefully fold in the rest of the egg whites.

Lay 12 crepes out on waxed paper, browned side up. Place 1 Tablespoon of the lemon souffléd mixture on the top half of each crepe and gently fold the lower half over it. Fold the crepes into quarters to make small triangles.

Arrange crépes side by side in a shallow buttered baking dish. Sprinkle each crêpe with a small amount of sugar. Bake on the middle shelf of the oven for 10 minutes or until they have puffed up and the sugar has melted.

Serve at once on heated plates, topped with Raspberry Sauce (see recipe on page 60). If made ahead, cover crêpes with plastic wrap and refrigerate. Allow to reach room temperature before baking.

Yield: 12 crepes

Raspberry Sauce

Use this Raspberry Sauce over Lemon Soufflé Crêpes or to top pound cake or ice cream. You can substitute strawberries for the raspberries, if you like.

   1   *10-ounce pack frozen raspberries, thawed*
   2   *teaspoons cornstarch*
   4   *Tablespoons Kirsch® or strawberry liqueur*

Drain berries, saving the juice. Combine the juice and cornstarch in a saucepan and stir over a low heat. When thickened, add liqueur and the berries. This sauce may be served warm or cold.

Creamy Creole Pralines

New Orleans famous candy — crunchy pecans in a creamy brown sugar candy.

   2   *cups granulated sugar*
   1   *cup brown sugar*
   1   *cup evaporated milk*
   2   *Tablespoons light or dark corn syrup*
$^1/_2$ *cup butter*
   1   *teaspoon vanilla*
   3   *cups pecans*

Put white and brown sugar, evaporated milk, and corn syrup in a heavy saucepan. Cook over medium-high heat for about 20 minutes or until the mixture reaches the soft ball stage, (236°F on a candy thermometer). If you do not have a candy thermometer, drop a small amount of the praline mixture into a cup of cold water. It should form a soft ball.

Remove from the heat and add butter. Beat with a wooden spoon until mixture is no longer shiny. Before the mixture becomes too thick, add vanilla and pecans. Mix well and drop by spoonfuls onto waxed paper.

Yield: 3-4 dozen candies

Pecan Sticks

These crunchy cookies are a family favorite.

- 1 cup unsalted butter, softened
- 1/4 cup sugar
- 2 cups flour
- 1/4 teaspoon salt
- 2 teaspoons vanilla extract
- 1 cup finely chopped pecans or other nuts
- 1 cup confectioners sugar, for garnish

Preheat oven to 350°.

In large mixing bowl, cream the softened butter with the sugar until light and fluffy. Add the flour and salt in three parts, mixing well after each addition. Beat in the vanilla and stir in the pecans. Chill dough 15-20 minutes.

Measure a tablespoon of dough, and shape into a cylinder about 2 inches long and 1/2 inch in diameter. Repeat until all dough is used. Arrange cookies about 1 inch apart on an ungreased cookie sheet or one that has been lined with parchment paper. Bake 10 to 12 minutes, or until they are a golden brown. Cool on wire racks and roll in the confectioners sugar.

Yield: 30 cookies

Louisiana Pecan Pie

A recipe for Southern pecan pie.

- 1/4 cup butter, softened
- 1 cup sugar
- 1 cup dark corn syrup
- 3 eggs
- 1 teaspoon vanilla
- dash salt
- 1 1/2 cups pecan halves
- 1 9" unbaked pie shell, page 57

Preheat oven 350°.

Using a wooden spoon, cream the butter with the sugar by hand (do not use an electric mixer). Add the corn syrup and cream well.

In a separate bowl beat the eggs with a whisk until they are light and lemon colored. Beat the eggs into the sugar mixture. Add vanilla, salt and pecans.

Pour into an unbaked 9" pie shell and bake at 350° for 45 minutes or until done. To test for doneness, insert knife in the center of the pie. It should come out with a clear syrup coating. Cool on a wire rack.

Yield: 1 pie, 6-8 servings

To Flame or Not To Flame

It isn't much fun to attempt to flame a dish and then have nothing happen at the big moment when the match is applied. The secret lies in having the food and the liqueur at the proper temperature before flaming. Both the food and the liqueur should be warm. An expert can pour the liqueur onto warm food and know precisely when to ignite it. Novices, however, can insure success by heating the liqueur separately in a small saucepan with a long handle. Take care to heat until just under the boiling point. Heating too high or for too long evaporates the alcohol. Ignite the liqueur in the pan, then pour it over your creation, or pour the warm liqueur over the dish and ignite it immediately.

Flamed Louisiana Peaches

A quick, easy, delicious dessert to make when you don't have much time.

       4 ripe fresh peaches, sliced
 ¹/4   cup butter
   2   Tablespoons Amaretto liqueur
   3   Tablespoons rum
       vanilla ice cream

In a chafing dish, sauté peaches in butter. Add Amaretto and stir well. Heat rum in a small saucepan, ignite, and pour over peaches. When flame subsides, serve over vanilla ice cream.
Yield: 6 servings

Bananas Foster

This dramatic dessert was created in New Orlean's famous Brennan's restaurant.

- ¹/₄ cup butter
- 2 heaping Tablespoons brown sugar
- 4 bananas
- 1 Tablespoon banana liqueur
  pinch cinnamon
- 1 Tablespoon rum
- 2 Tablespoons brandy
  vanilla ice cream

   Mix butter and brown sugar in a large skillet or chafing dish. Cook over medium heat until sugar melts. Slice bananas in halves or quarters and add to the butter mixture, cooking until they are heated through. Add liqueur and cinnamon and stir. Sprinkle rum and brandy over the top. DO NOT STIR. Ignite. Spoon gently a few times. Serve warm over vanilla ice cream.
   Yield: 6 servings

Café Brûlot

Serve this coffee in your prettiest demitasse cups. Almost a dessert in itself.

       1   cup cognac or brandy
       2   ounces orange Curacao (optional)
       1   Tablespoon whole cloves
       2   sticks cinnamon, broken
     1/2   orange thinly sliced and quartered
     1/2   lemon thinly sliced and quartered
      24   sugar lumps
       1   quart very strong black coffee

In a small saucepan, heat brandy and Curacao over a low flame just until it gets hot. Place cloves, cinnamon, orange, lemon slices, and sugar lumps in a Brûlot bowl or chafing dish. Pour warm brandy into the bowl and ignite. Flame for 3 to 4 minutes. Pour in the strong hot coffee and stir well to dissolve the sugar.
Yield: 12 demitasse cup servings

Café Au Lait

A must with the French Market doughnuts, page 50.

       2   cups strong black-dripped coffee, preferably
           Louisiana coffee or a dark French Roast
       2   cups milk heated
           sugar to taste

Pour each cup half full of coffee; add an equal amount of milk. Sweeten to taste.
Yield: 4 servings